TIME IN KAFKA

Len Jenkin

BROADWAY PLAY PUBLISHING INC
224 E 62nd St, NY, NY 10065
www.broadwayplaypub.com
info@broadwayplaypub.com

First printing: August 2012
Second printing: December 2014

I S B N: 978-0-88145-531-1

Book design: Marie Donovan
Page make-up: Adobe Indesign
Typeface: Palatino
Printed and bound in the U S A

TIME IN KAFKA was first produced by the
Undermain Theater in Dallas. It opened on 5
February 2012 with the following players and creative
contributors:

Anne Beyer
Jessica Cavanagh
Ricco Fajardo
Blake Hackler
Martha Harms
Shannon Kearns-Simmons
Anthony L Ramirez
Dennis Raveneau
Teddy Spencer
Paul Taylor
Rachael Werline

Director..Katherine Owens
Production design......................John Arnone, Giva Taylor,
Steve Woods, Bruce DuBose,
Robert Winn, & Jeffrey Franks

CHARACTERS

JAY SPELLMAN, *a literary man*
PROFESSOR FELDMAN, *another literary man*
COUNT FOSCO, *an encounter*
GENERAL DEVRIES, *a soldier, retired*
HAROLD BOOTHBY, *a man of the world*
DR HARTUNGEN, *director of the clinic*
FRANZ KAFKA, *the insurance officer from Prague*
DESKCLERK, *a servant of the clinic*
DIANE SPELLMAN, JAY's *wife*
PRINCIPESSA STURDZA, *perhaps a Gypsy*
CHARLOTTE, *a close associate of* BOOTHBY'S
ANNA, *a young woman*
EMILIA, *a servant of the clinic*

SETTING

Time: now, and then

Place: A transit terminal that echoes a 19th century European railway station (Saint Pancras, Gare du Nord) —iron arches and vaulting, a bar, a railway hotel entry, train platforms somewhere. This set transforms into whatever location is required without ever disappearing entirely. Above, a large departure board.

Places: JAY SPELLMAN's *lecture room*
DIANE *and* JAY SPELLMAN's *bedroom*
Train from Milan to Desenzano
Ferryboat
The harbor at Riva
Bar Centrale, Milano
At the Clinic: Consulting room
The Sunroom on the lake
A Pier
Music Room
Reception
Dining Room

Thanks to Franz Kafka, W G Sebald, and Guy Davenport. Brilliant work, gentlemen. I stand in your long shadows.

This one is for Emily

1.

(*On the departure board:* **The Clinic/A New Patient***)*

(KAFKA *in deep shadow, barely visible, jacket and tie, suitcase.*)

(*Pieces of the clinic appear. The* DESKCLERK's *table. A piano. Medical charts. Racks of herbal remedies*)

(*The* DESKCLERK *walks out to his table. On it is a bell, a microphone, an overhead projector, a pile of papers, postcards, pictures. Behind him is a row of boxes, some with letters in them, or room keys.*)

(*The* DESKCLERK *fishes around in the pile of papers, tries some in the overhead projector: page of a medical journal, a group doing calisthenics, an exercise instruction chart. Then a blurry black and white image...*)

(*Projection: a sprawling building overlooking a lake. Soothing music*)

(*The* DESKCLERK *sits, notices* KAFKA, *speaks into his microphone.*)

DESKCLERK: (*Into mike*) Welcome to the clinic.

(KAFKA *takes a hesitant step forward.*)

DESKCLERK: Name? Name?

2.

(On the Departure Board: **Assistant Professor Spellman/ The bridegroom will never get to his wedding/a college, U S A***)*

(Professor JAY SPELLMAN *lectures to his freshman class.)*

SPELLMAN: Joseph K will never discover what crimes condemn him to death. The eager bridegroom will never get to his wedding in the country. The ship of the hunter Gracchus will never get its bearings, forever lost between death and life. Time in Kafka is always broken. Every moment leads back to itself, infinite with echoes, chronological and eternal.

Any questions from the peanut gallery? Then that's it, boys and girls. Start your essays on *The Trial.* Next week, same time, same station-- though of course, some of us may never actually get here.

3.

(Departure board: **Assistant Professor Spellman's office/ The streets of Prague***)*

(One wall is covered with a streetmap of Prague in the early 1900's, a huge blow-up marked with arrows and symbols. SPELLMAN *is with* DEAN FELDMAN, *an older professor.)*

SPELLMAN: Look, Arthur, you did brilliant work on Kafka before I finished high school—I respect that work—but the key to that tubercular Jew—you missed completely.

DEAN FELDMAN: Did I now?

SPELLMAN: You looked brilliantly—in all the wrong places.

DEAN FELDMAN: Jay, I didn't come to your office to argue Kafka. I have something I need to discuss that...

SPELLMAN: *(Pointing to map)* The ring road that circles Prague. His apartment house, Yiddish Theater, the Accident Insurance office building. Probably condos by now. Kafka's daily walk through the old ghetto took him counter-clockwise—

(The street and house names appear on the departure board as SPELLMAN *says them.)*

SPELLMAN: Lassovskaia, Staromestska, Street of the Black Madonna, Street of the Golden Bears. The deliberate route Kafka followed reveals that he...

DEAN FELDMAN: Jay, do you realize that your students are freshmen? They should be writing essays on George Orwell, or their new sexual orientation. They're eighteen, for God's sake.

SPELLMAN: What are you talking about?

DEAN FELDMAN: I've warned you often enough. The college doesn't pay you to deliver arcane lectures about Kafka that fly a few miles over...

SPELLMAN: I'm their teacher, Arthur. I will not be responsible for shoveling pedestrian shit into their heads.

DEAN FELDMAN: In that case, I'm afraid you're fired. As of now. Staley can take over your classes.

SPELLMAN: Staley is a moron.

DEAN FELDMAN: True enough. Good luck.

SPELLMAN: Wait a fucking minute here.

DEAN FELDMAN: I feel sorry for your wife. Diane deserves someone with a better sense of...

SPELLMAN: ALL RIGHT! I'll teach the damn freshmen anyway you...

DEAN FELDMAN: You've said that before, Jay. If you need a reference, get it from someone else.

SPELLMAN: We live here. Diane is still paying off college loans.

DEAN FELDMAN: My responsibility is to our students.

SPELLMAN: I've got a mortgage, Arthur.

DEAN FELDMAN: That's not my affair.

SPELLMAN: What am I supposed to do?

DEAN FELDMAN: Clear out your office.
By the way, your ideas about Kafka are out on the ledge. Professional suicidal. Nonsense. *(He leaves.)*

SPELLMAN: *(Calling after him)* Can I get a break here?

4.

(Departure board: **One week later/Jay and Diane Spellman's house/ mental garbage***)*

(A double bed, and DIANE SPELLMAN *has fallen asleep on it, in her clothes. Her cellphone rings. She wakes, fumbles for it...)*

DIANE: Jay? Jay? JAY! Thank God! Where the fuck are you? ...Of course you woke me. It's 4 A M. I've been waiting up for you every night. You just disappeared, dammit.

(In another space, Jay Spellman. He's in a train compartment, cellphone in hand.)

SPELLMAN: I couldn't help it, Diane.

DIANE: Jay, I've been going nuts. The cops were here. They're still looking for you.

SPELLMAN: I had this dream...

DIANE: Dream? You're fucking kidding, right? Car's gone, you're gone. I don't hear a word for days. I'm thinking you ran off with one of your students, and then Arthur called to tell me he'd fired you and I didn't know what to think. They dragged the fucking lake. Are you...

SPELLMAN: I'm fine. I'm sorry. I'm so sorry. I forgot to call. I forgot everything. The car's in a parking garage at the airport.

DIANE: Airport? Where the hell are you?

SPELLMAN: Listen, Diane. The night I was fired, he came to me. In a dream. Kafka.

(KAFKA *crawls out from under* DIANE'*s bed, looking like himself, but covered with a silvery dust.*)

SPELLMAN: He slid out from under our bed, covered with dust, as if he'd been there for years.

(KAFKA *gets into bed with* DIANE. *She can't see him.*)

SPELLMAN: He smelled like herring. He spoke German.

DIANE: You don't even know German.

SPELLMAN: In my dream I understood every word.

(KAFKA *speaks, in English.* DIANE *has her cell to her ear.* SPELLMAN *rides the train, talking into his cellphone...*)

KAFKA: In September 1913, I traveled to the International Congress for Accident Prevention in Vienna. I spent three days there in the Hotel Royale, sleepless, with a migraine, staring at the cracks in the ceiling of my room. I continued by rail, via Trieste to Desenzano, then by ferry to Riva and the clinic, where I hoped the nature therapies would heal my lungs.

(*Departure board reads:* #241 Rapido-Trieste-Desenzano-Monte Carlo)

(DIANE *gets out of bed, taking the cellphone.* KAFKA *remains in the bed, sitting up.*)

KAFKA: In Trieste, at the Hotel Linzerhof, I encountered a Polish chambermaid, whose sexual appetites....

SPELLMAN: Stop right there. You can't be here, in my dream, to tell me you bonked some chambermaid. There's gotta be...

KAFKA: There is. I wrote a book. A book about Joseph L, an actor in the Yiddish theater, the Prophet Elijah, and Bisi and Kisi, the twin daughters of a Czech nobleman, Prince Sikarov. A monumental failure-- senseless tangle of lust and religion, and yet I couldn't feed it to the flames. I left the manuscript....

(KAFKA's *voice blurs as he pulls the covers over his head disappearing into a pile of bedding.* SPELLMAN *continues the narrative....*)

SPELLMAN: Kafka told me he left the manuscript at a sanatorium, the Hartungen Naturopathic Clinic, run by a Doctor Hartungen. It's in a town on a lake, Riva del Garda.
He stayed there for a few weeks...

DIANE: A hundred years ago. You're gonna go there, aren't you, Jay? To Riva del Garda, wherever the hell that is.

SPELLMAN: Italy. I'm on a train. We must be near Verona by now.

DIANE: Verona?

SPELLMAN: I flew to Milan.

DIANE: I can't believe this. I can't believe you.

SPELLMAN: Diane, listen to me.

DIANE: I'm listening, Jay. God knows why.

SPELLMAN: If I find this unknown Kafka novel, I will become the unfireable professor. We go to Harvard, double the salary. We can...

DIANE: Jay, you're crazy.

SPELLMAN: I'm gonna find it, Diane.

DIANE: Jay, people have dreams, they forget them and go about their business. Dreams are not good advice, Jay. They're mental garbage.

SPELLMAN: I'm hanging up now.

DIANE: Does this clinic even still exist?

SPELLMAN: It exists. Or records exist. Or...

DIANE: Jay...I love you.

SPELLMAN: I love you too.

DIANE: Then get to an airport and come home. Please. We can...

SPELLMAN: I'm hanging up now.

(MR BOOTHBY, *forties, enters* SPELLMAN's *train compartment with* CHARLOTTE, *a much younger woman.*)

BOOTHBY: Are these seats unoccupied? May we...

SPELLMAN: Sure. *(He closes his cellphone, hanging up.)*

DIANE: *(Into cellphone)* Jay? JAY? Fuck. *(She hangs up, then redials her cell.)* The number for Alitalia Airlines, please.

5.

(Departure board: **Montague & Boothby Ltd., Rare Books, Autographs, Ephemera.***)*

*(*BOOTHBY *and* CHARLOTTE *settle into* SPELLMAN's *train compartment.*)*

BOOTHBY: Thank you for allowing us to share your compartment, my dear sir. I'm Boothby, Harold Boothby. This is my niece, Charlotte. Charlotte, say hello to the gentleman.

CHARLOTTE: Hello.

BOOTHBY: And as the caterpillar said, sir, who are you?

SPELLMAN: Jay Spellman.

BOOTHBY: American?

SPELLMAN: Is it that obvious?

BOOTHBY: *(Sings)* "Give me land, lots of land, 'neath the starry skies above, Don't fence me in..." What do you do in those wide open spaces?

SPELLMAN: I'm a professor. Of Comparative Literature.

BOOTHBY: I admire you, sir. I admire you.

SPELLMAN: Assistant professor, actually.

BOOTHBY: I'm an ignorant man. I dreamed of attending Oxford, but I had to earn my living. One of those unfortunates who knows the price of everything and the value of nothing. I'm a bookdealer. Montague and Boothby, rare editions. Montague's been dead for twenty years. I carry on alone. Charlotte is a student. She attends a very private school in the mountains.

CHARLOTTE: Saint Helena's. You get there by cable car, over the glaciers. Women only. I'm between terms.

SPELLMAN: What are you studying at...

CHARLOTTE: All the girls are ferocious lesbots. The dormitory lounge is a scene out of the third circle of...

BOOTHBY: Charlotte! Behave yourself. Stop telling the professor such lies.

CHARLOTTE: Where are you traveling to?

SPELLMAN: Riva, on Lake Garda. There's a clinic I need to go to. For...stress

BOOTHBY: What a coincidence. That's exactly where we're going.

CHARLOTTE: Healing baths.

BOOTHBY: Herbal cocktails.

CHARLOTTE: Emilia may already be polishing the doorknob.

SPELLMAN: Excuse me?

(CHARLOTTE *lights a cigarette.*)

CHARLOTTE: Do you mind if I smoke?

BOOTHBY: Are you aware, sir, that during the war, this very rail line was used by the Nazis as the main transport for prisoners in this area. In '44 these tracks were lined with boxcars packed with naked Jews. The boxcars were hauled to Desenzano on Lago de Garda, where they were rolled onto ferries. The ferries steamed out to the middle of the lake. The cars were pushed overboard, full with mothers, fathers, children, rabbis, thieves, whores, peddlers, doctors, shoemakers, bialy bakers—all sank to the bottom of the lake. They're still there, a long train of the dead without a locomotive. Fish swim by their eyes.

6.

(*Departure board:* **The Lake Ferry: Desenzano-Sirmione-Riva del Garda**)

(SPELLMAN *on board with a suitcase. Other travelers. Italian traveling music.*)

(*Boat horn*)

SPELLMAN: Those people I met on the train don't seem to be on board. I wonder how they're...

CAPTAIN: (*O S*) Rive del Garda!

(EMILIA *appears, a middle-aged woman, polishing the brass doorknob of an imposing old-fashioned door.*)

SPELLMAN: The harbor at Riva. Two boys play at dice near the ferry dock. A Turkish girl sells figs under the arcade.

CAPTAIN: *(O S)* Did you say figs, or pigs?

SPELLMAN: The owner of a lakeside cafe puts his head down on a table and dreams. A woman is polishing a doorknob. A flock of doves bursts suddenly from a rooftop...

CAPTAIN: *(O S) Basta!* Get off the boat!

(SPELLMAN does. Unsure of where to go, he approaches EMILIA...)

SPELLMAN: *Bongiorno.* I just arrived. On that ferry. I need to find a clinic. It was here in Riva a long time ago, and I thought maybe...

EMILIA: Do you have an appointment?

SPELLMAN: Appointment?

EMILIA With Doctor Hartungen.

SPELLMAN: Hartungen? You actually said "Doctor Hartungen."

EMILIA: Of course. He's the clinic director.

SPELLMAN: No he's not. He's dead. He's been dead for ninety years.

EMILIA: Someone is playing a joke with you, *signore.*

SPELLMAN: You are.

(EMILIA opens the door wide for SPELLMAN.)

EMILIA: See the deskclerk. Straight ahead, then left, second right past the fountain, up the marble staircase, then follow the signs to... *(She's gone.)*

7.

(On the departure board: **The clinic/a new patient***)*

(Projection: the sprawling building overlooking the lake. Soothing music)

(The clinic re-appears, this time around SPELLMAN. *The piano. The eyechart. Racks of herbal remedies. The* DESKCLERK's *table, exactly as in Scene 1, with a bell, a microphone, an overhead projector, a pile of papers, postcards, pictures...)*

(The DESKCLERK, *at his table, notices* SPELLMAN, *speaks into his microphone.)*

DESKCLERK: *(Into mike)* Welcome to the clinic. Name?

SPELLMAN: Spellman.

(The DESKCLERK *hunts through his pile of papers, finally finding the one he wants.)*

DESKCLERK: Ah. *(He looks the paper over, then puts it aside.)* How long will you be with us?

SPELLMAN: I don't know. It depends how I...

DESKCLERK: Length of stay—unknown.
This afternoon, examinations and the prescription. Your naturopathic healing regimen. Diet, breathing, calisthenics. Herbs. Emilia will have your schedule. No smoking.

SPELLMAN: Look, I just need to see the director.

DESKCLERK: Doctor Hartungen? That's impossible. He's...

DR HARTUNGEN: appears in a white doctor's coat, with Emilia.

EMILIA: Doctor, this gentleman insists you're already in your grave.

DR HARTUNGEN: Does he now?

SPELLMAN: Whoever you are, you're not Doctor Hartungen. Hartungen was practicing medicine here in 1913. He'd be almost a hundred years old.

DR HARTUNGEN: Join me in my consulting room, Mister...

DESKCLERK: Spellman. Professor Spellman. Length of stay unknown.

DR HARTUNGEN: ...Professor Spellman, and you can be the judge of whether or not I've died...

8.

(Departure Board: **The Consulting Room/Hartungen Naturopathic Clinic/Riva del Garda***)*

(Chairs, a skeleton. SPELLMAN *and* DR HARTUNGEN*)*

DR HARTUNGEN: My grandfather founded this clinic. He died in 1921. My father became chief physician and director for many years. I am the present Doctor Hartungen...a family business.

SPELLMAN: My apologies. I'm just having a hard time believing the Hartungen Naturopathic Clinic still exists. I imagined I might find an apartment building on the clinic site. Or a disco. You're not listed anywhere.

DR HARTUNGEN: We operate privately.
Now tell me—why have you come here? Are you ill?

SPELLMAN: Doctor, this will sound crazy but—there was something left behind by a patient. Almost a century ago. 1913, in the fall.
The patient was a Doctor Kafka.

DR HARTUNGEN: Kafka? Not a name I know. Swiss? Austrian?

SPELLMAN: A German Jew from Prague. A writer. He's become quite famous since then.

DR HARTUNGEN: Not to me. My work here keeps me occupied, and we have little contact with the world outside. No newspapers, television, computers. They agitate the nerves of the patients.
Are you a relative of this Kafka?

SPELLMAN: I'm a...professor of literature. A scholar. I believe Kafka left a manuscript here, a book.

DR HARTUNGEN: Many patients abandon things here-- letters, photographs, private papers. The Hartungen policy has always been, from our founding, to never throw anything away.

SPELLMAN: My God! Wonderful!

DR HARTUNGEN: There are storage areas in the natural tunnels that honeycomb the rock beneath the clinic.

SPELLMAN: Please, doctor. This is important. To me. To the world. Can you search for the book?

DR HARTUNGEN: It may take some time.

SPELLMAN: You'll do it! Thank you! Thank you!

DR HARTUNGEN: Even if we find it, it may have been damaged by age...

SPELLMAN: That book will be in the window of every Barnes and Noble, number one on Amazon...

DR HARTUNGEN: ...the tunnels are damp.

SPELLMAN: ...with my intro and commentary...

DR HARTUNGEN: Then there are the rats.

SPELLMAN: ...translated into Chinese, Spanish, Hungarian...

DR HARTUNGEN: The hotels along the lakeshore are closed for the season. It will be my pleasure to give you a room here, and your meals.

SPELLMAN: I don't know what to say.

I hope I won't be imposing on your hospitality for too long.

DR HARTUNGEN: The search will certainly begin tomorrow, or the day after. The tunnels are low-ceilinged, and extensive. Emilia will need to gather small children from the village, provide them with electric torches. We will find this Kafka's manuscript. Eventually. Follow me.

(DR HARTUNGEN *and* SPELLMAN *cross to the* DESKCLERK's *area.*)

DR HARTUNGEN: Feel free to use the sunroom, the baths, herbal...

SPELLMAN: *(Checking his pockets)* I seem to have lost my cellphone.

DR HARTUNGEN: Just as well. They don't work here.

DESKCLERK: The wind off the lake. It blows the calls astray.

SPELLMAN: I need to call the states. My wife...

DR HARTUNGEN: We have no telephones.

SPELLMAN: Let me guess. They agitate the nerves.

DR HARTUNGEN: Indeed. You can send a telegram, of course.

DESKCLERK: The telegraph office is in the village, Piazza Brolo, under the arcade. It opens every Monday at noon for an hour.

DR HARTUNGEN: If Signore Bustamante hasn't gone to visit his sister in Bolzano.

(*As* DR HARTUNGEN *exits, the* PRINCIPESSA STURDZA *enters. Alongside her is* ANNA)

STURDZA: We've been expecting you. I foresaw your arrival, in the cards.

SPELLMAN: The cards?

DESKCLERK: Professor Spellman, your fellow patients...

SPELLMAN: I'm not a pat..

DESKCLERK: ...the Principessa Sturdza, and...

ANNA: And I'm Anna.

STURDZA: My protege. I'm teaching Anna to dance, to tame wild horses, and to steal.

ANNA: Pay no attention to her. She drank an entire bottle of champagne at the lake.

STURDZA: I never drink. Anna is lying to you, professor.

ANNA: Am not.

STURDZA: And why does she lie? She's jealous of me, because...

ANNA: Ridiculous.

STURDZA: ...because she is too young to understand men like you.

SPELLMAN: Men like me? What can you know about me?

STURDZA: Ah. You pretend to an interest in literature and things of the mind, but when I came into this room you ran your eyes over my body, my large breasts. You thought, in spite of her age, this woman remains extremely attractive. She has mystery. She would be far more interesting in bed than any naive young girl.

SPELLMAN: Principessa, you read my mind perfectly.

STURDZA: You see, Anna, I have already made him lie. Who can say what I will make him do next?

DESKCLERK: The dinner bell rings at seven. Like this. (*He rings his bell.*)

STURDZA: Idiot. Professor Spellman, no matter how serious the problem that brings you here, it's not too late.

SPELLMAN: I damn well hope so.

STURDZA: Remember Lazarus. *(Checking her watch)* Anna, you should be doing your...

ANNA: I don't care.

STURDZA: Don't be foolish, child.

(STURDZA takes ANNA's arm. They turn to go.)

ANNA: We'll see you there, I hope.

DESKCLERK: EMILIA!

STURDZA: Where?

SPELLMAN: Dinner. Today is Friday. The small fishes from the lake, cooked in white wine.

(ANNA and STURDZA are gone. EMILIA enters, picks up SPELLMAN's suitcase.)

SPELLMAN: He had a good doctor.

EMILIA: Who?

SPELLMAN: Lazarus.

EMILIA: Indeed he did. Follow me.

SPELLMAN: Some patients seem to think this place is a party. Or a joke.

EMILIA: Would you rather they pitied you? Should they weep? Poor...

DESKCLERK: Professor Spellman.

EMILIA: ...Professor Spellman. He's ill, just like everyone else who comes here. He's dying, just like...

SPELLMAN: Actually, I didn't come here because I'm sick. I came here to...

DESKCLERK: East wing, third floor, corridor six.

EMILIA: Very nice. Lake view. Follow me.

(Off EMILIA *and* SPELLMAN *go.)*

DESKCLERK: *(To audience)* Welcome to the clinic. Good luck. Did I say no smoking?

9.

(Departure Board: **Resto-bar, Hotel Centrale, Milano/ Come here often?***)*

*(*DIANE *at a hotel bar in Milan, along with the* BARMAN *and* COUNT FOSCO.*)*

DIANE: *(To* BARMAN*)* Kir, *per favore.*

COUNT FOSCO: Come here often?

DIANE: You must be kidding.

COUNT FOSCO: Not at all.

DIANE: At least you speak English.

COUNT FOSCO: I went to school in America.

DIANE: Really? Where?

COUNT FOSCO: Harvard. They kicked me out. Drugs. Just as well. My family was running out of money. They had to sell sixty acres of olive trees to keep me in Elliot House. Not worth it, believe me.

(The BARMAN *delivers* DIANE's *kir.)*

COUNT FOSCO: On my tab, *per favore*

(The BARMAN *nods, and he's gone.)*

DIANE: Are you trying to pick me up?

COUNT FOSCO: Perish the thought, Madonna.

DIANE: Well then, what's a Harvard man doing hanging around the bar of a second-rate hotel?

COUNT FOSCO: A young lady was to meet me here an hour ago. I believe she changed her mind. They often do. Call me Fosco. Everyone does. My actual name is Count Armando Foscarelli.

DIANE: Diane Spellman.

COUNT FOSCO: Now that we've introduced ourselves, let's go up to your room.

DIANE: I don't think so.

COUNT FOSCO: Madonna, Fosco does not offer twice. There are other tourists with euros in their purses.

DIANE: I'm not a tourist. I'm trying to find my husband.

COUNT FOSCO: A large thing to lose, Madonna.

DIANE: He's chasing Kafka.

COUNT FOSCO: He's not the first.

DIANE: I need to go to Riva del Garda in the morning.

COUNT FOSCO: Very sleepy place this time of year. If your missing husband went there, he made a poor travel choice. Stay in Milano with me, Madonna. We could...

DIANE: How do I find the train station?

COUNT FOSCO: Say to the taxi *"Ferrovaria Centrale."* I leave you to your kir, and your loss.
Perhaps you will give me some money?

DIANE: For what?

COUNT FOSCO: For my company, signora, and my advice.

DIANE What advice?

COUNT FOSCO: Men are worthless, and as numerous as blades of grass in the fields. The differences between them are small at best. They have no thoughts of their own, no passion, no integrity.

DIANE: You don't know my husband.

COUNT FOSCO: So true, Madonna. But I doubt he'd change my opinion.

DIANE: Are you the shining exception?

COUNT FOSCO: Not at all. I am as empty as a chair. As a bird.
You were wise not to do fucking with Fosco. For the woman, a bad feeling after, like a sour taste in the soul. *(He holds out a hand, palm up. He waits for euros.)*

COUNT FOSCO: I have to live.

(DIANE offers nothing, sips her kir. He shrugs.)

COUNT FOSCO: Fosco won't say goodbye. We may meet again. *Ciao*, Madonna. *(He's gone.)*

10.

(Departure board: **In the Music Room Dr. Hartungen and General Devries***)*

(Music— Chopin)

(The Music Room, as ANNA *plays piano. On the piano, a lit candelabra.* GENERAL DEVRIES *in his wheelchair is nearby. He reads. His feet are bare.)*

(Projection: Sheet music. The DESKCLERK *turns the pages for* ANNA *when its time.)*

DESKCLERK: Meanwhile, in the Music Room, Anna plays Chopin's Etude number six, the Dancing Soldier.

DEVRIES: *(Reading)* The dreary intercourse of daily life, shall ne'er prevail against us...

DESKCLERK: General Devries. He's been here at the clinic since the war. EMILIA!

(EMILIA *comes on with a washbasin, kneels and begins to wash* DEVRIES's *feet.)*

(DR HARTUNGEN *enters, goes to* DEVRIES.*)*

DR HARTUNGEN: General, I'm afraid your daughter still refuses to pay your bills—six months now.

DEVRIES: I really don't care, Doctor. Put me out on the street. I'll beg at the ferry dock.

DR HARTUNGEN: A brilliant plan. I'll have them give you a tin cup from the kitchen. *(Looking at General's open book)* What's the poem?

DEVRIES: Tintern Abbey. Wordsworth. He suits me these days. I'll read you....just a moment...

(DEVRIES *searches his book for a quotation. As he does so,* ANNA *stops playing suddenly. She walks over to a window, looks out.)*

(*Projection: The sheet music is gone, replaced by the lake, night. A ferry in the distance, its windows lit, moving across the water.)*

DEVRIES: "The dreary intercourse of daily life,
Shall e'er prevail against us, or disturb
Our cheerful faith, that all which we behold
Is full of blessings...."

DR HARTUNGEN: Not quite all. A new patient, a young man, only seventeen, arrived last night. He didn't come down to breakfast, his bed hadn't been slept in. We found him this evening in the woods, halfway up the hillside toward Alto Adige. He'd shot himself through the temple.

DEVRIES: Pity.

DR HARTUNGEN: A small animal was tearing at his face. It ran off as we approached. A fox, I believe.

DEVRIES: I've seen battlefields thick with corpses. Dogs and crows rip at the bodies, pulling flesh from bone.

Old women make their slow way among the dead,
slide wedding rings off cold fingers.

DR HARTUNGEN: General, I believe that God has at last
abandoned us.

DEVRIES: Nonsense.

DR HARTUNGEN: He's left us crouching by this lake in
the dark, too frightened to..

DEVRIES: God won't abandon us, Doctor—though he
may not always hover above the church in a golden
cloud. Do you know more than God about who should
live and who should die? Do you know how best to
feed his foxes?

(EMILIA *wipes off* DEVRIES'*s feet, puts his slippers on him.*)

EMILIA: There. Done.

DEVRIES: Thank you, Emilia. You're so kind.

EMILIA: It was nothing. Goodnight, General.
Goodnight, Doctor

(*A silence between them.*)

DR HARTUNGEN: I believe I won't send you begging at
the ferry after all. Do you take the baths?

DEVRIES: I'm not strong enough.

DR HARTUNGEN: Are you doing your breathing by the
lake?

DEVRIES: Not for a month.

DR HARTUNGEN: Begin again. I'll have Emilia walk you
down to the cabins tomorrow. Goodnight.

DEVRIES: Goodnight, Doctor.

DR HARTUNGEN: I'll write your daughter about the
bill...

DEVRIES: Do that. And give that child my love.

(DR HARTUNGEN *leaves.* DEVRIES *returns to his book.*
ANNA *returns to the piano, begins to play again, this time
its a simple melody, played hesitantly, picked out with one
finger. She picks up the candelabra, goes over to the general.
He's asleep over his book. The candelabra in one hand, and
pushing the wheelchair with the other, she and* DEVRIES
exit.)

11.

(*Departure board:* **In the Sunroom/Harold Boothby gets
serious**)

(*The* DESKCLERK *pulls the slide of the clinic off the projector,
inserts a new image.*)

(*Projection: a skeleton reading a book.*)

(*The Sunroom appears, an arrangement of lounge chairs.*
SPELLMAN *enters with a book.*)

(CHARLOTTE *is nearby, finishing her make-up. She dials her
cell.*)

CHARLOTTE: *(On cell)* Hi, babe. Look, I need to talk to
you, but I'm about to go on here... Yeah, I'm still doing
the clinic thing... So its weird, so what? ...Bobby, there's
no nudity. ...Not everyone can afford to sit around and
be an artist... Look, as soon as I get a break I'll...

DESKCLERK: Some hours later, or is it days...

CHARLOTTE: *(On cell)* Love you. Gotta go.

(CHARLOTTE *closes her cell, she's gone.* SPELLMAN *sits,
reads.*)

DESKCLERK: In any case, some time later, Professor
Spellman has wandered into the Sunroom. While
waiting for the manuscript search to begin, he studies
the methods of the clinic.

(SPELLMAN *shows us his book.*)

SPELLMAN: *Healing Secrets of Nature,* by Doctor Hermann Hartungen, published Milan, 1923.

(SPELLMAN reads. BOOTHBY and CHARLOTTE enter the sunroom.)

BOOTHBY: Are these lounge chairs occupied? May we...

SPELLMAN: Of course.

BOOTHBY: Thank you for allowing us to share this therapeutic chamber, my dear sir. We met on the train. Say hello to the gentleman, Charlotte.

CHARLOTTE: Hello.

BOOTHBY: Charlotte is my occasional traveling companion. I pay her handsomely, but I'm afraid she finds my stays at the clinic boring. The stress of the book business takes its toll, sir. The kidneys.

CHARLOTTE: Boothby's not sick. He likes the attention.

BOOTHBY: A palpable falsehood.

CHARLOTTE: The nursing.

BOOTHBY: There's blood in my urine.

CHARLOTTE: The drugs. Some kind of herb. He triples the dose.

BOOTHBY: Charlotte can be far too casual about the sufferings of others.

SPELLMAN: I didn't see you on the ferry...

BOOTHBY: Travel over water disagrees with me. The mal-de-mer...

(CHARLOTTE lights a cigarette.)

CHARLOTTE: We hitch-hiked. Boothby's broke. We couldn't afford ferry tickets.
Do you mind if I smoke?

SPELLMAN: Isn't it against the...

CHARLOTTE: Would you like one?

DESKCLERK: Charlotte smokes mentholated hashish. She gets high and cool-- simultaneously.

CHARLOTTE: Shut up. Idiot.

BOOTHBY: I don't mean to pry, Professor Spellman, but you appear to be a robust, virile sort of man. Why are you here?

SPELLMAN: At the clinic?

CHARLOTTE: Are you some kind of moron? Where else?

SPELLMAN: I have cancer. It's spread from the pancreas to the lymph nodes. Inoperable. I have a month, maybe two. Unless this place provides a miracle.

CHARLOTTE: What are lymph nodes?

SPELLMAN: They're the little things that...

CHARLOTTE: Ignore that question. I have a better one. Do you want to live?

SPELLMAN: What do you mean?

CHARLOTTE: What I said. Life isn't all it's cracked up to be.

BOOTHBY: Your interest in his cancer, Charlotte, ironic as it may be, is wasted. There's been a serious misdiagnosis. Or Professor Spellman is lying to us.

SPELLMAN: Think what you like.

BOOTHBY: I always do.

(*A silence between them.* CHARLOTTE *smokes. She takes out a copy of Kafka's* The Trial.)

SPELLMAN: You're reading Kafka.

CHARLOTTE: For lit class. *The Trial.*

SPELLMAN: I teach that book.

CHARLOTTE: There's nothing to teach. It's an instruction manual.

SPELLMAN: Instruction? For what?

CHARLOTTE: How to be paranoid. *(She kisses her copy of* The Trial, *then holds it up reverently.)* The Paranoid Bible.

SPELLMAN: That's not paranoia. It's prophecy. Kafka's a historian. The terrors he described hadn't happened yet. Then they did. And they will again.

BOOTHBY: Very clever, Professor Spellman, but that doesn't make it true.

CHARLOTTE: Why does Joseph K. say he doesn't know what his crimes are?

SPELLMAN: Because he doesn't.

CHARLOTTE: He's lying.

SPELLMAN: That's ridiculous. I've studied Kafka for...

CHARLOTTE: Everybody knows what their crimes are. Don't we?

BOOTHBY: Professor Spellman, are you, by any chance, a bookdealer?

SPELLMAN: Bookdealer? No. I'm...

BOOTHBY: Then I can be honest with you. There are rumours afoot of a potential literary discovery that will rock the publishing world. A lost work of Franz Kafka. The book is supposedly set in a mirror version of Prague, involving a lust crazed Rabbi, Joseph M, and a singularly well-endowed Yiddish theater actress, the enigmatic Sasha Finkelstein.
A literary scholar like yourself, perhaps you have some special knowledge of this manuscript?

SPELLMAN: I never heard of it.

BOOTHBY: Of course not. *(He begins doing strange calisthenics.)*

DESKCLERK: This morning Mister Boothby mixed his herbs for the week into one dose. They sing in his blood. He performs Doctor Hartungen's Seven Postures of the Mongoose to stimulate his internal organs, the kidneys in particular.

(BOOTHBY pauses, holding a pose. CHARLOTTE stretches, lights another cigarette. SPELLMAN can't help staring at her. BOOTHBY relaxes.)

BOOTHBY: You admire Charlotte, Professor Spellman?

SPELLMAN: Doesn't everyone?

CHARLOTTE: Fucking sexist morons.

BOOTHBY: Charlotte! There's no call for that kind of talk.
Poor girl. Her parents died in the war, a stray shell right through the roof of the barn. They were potato farmers near Minsk, innocent potato farmers.

SPELLMAN: What war? She must be twenty. What war are you talking about?

BOOTHBY: Professor Spellman, one mustn't be too curious when it comes to wars. Unfortunate affairs.

(Projection: A chart of healing dance instruction, illustrated with the outlines of footprints.)

DESKCLERK: *(On mike)* Healing dance number six.

(Music. BOOTHBY and CHARLOTTE dance. So does everyone else. Fabulous finish. Music ends. BOOTHBY turns to SPELLMAN.)

BOOTHBY: Join me on the pier over the lake. The night sky, the lights of the little villages across the water, the silhouette of the abandoned church...

(BOOTHBY *and* SPELLMAN *exit, arm in arm.* CHARLOTTE *remains as lights fade in the sunroom. She takes out her cell.)*

CHARLOTTE: *(On cell)* Hello? Hello...pick up, dammit.... Your message is so fucking annoying. I'm sorry I said that. I'm a little stressed here... *(And on under the* DESKCLERK's *song)*

(The DESKCLERK *stands, takes his mike. Music. He sings.)*

DESKCLERK: *(Sings)*
Traveling on, my children, traveling on
Below the waters of the lake, traveling on
Up along the starry sky,
We will get there by and by,
Traveling on, my children, traveling on...

CHARLOTTE: *(On cell)* ...Look, I'll meet you at that Indian place as soon as I get through this damn thing... the Deskclerk singing, something about his children. Look, Bobby, who cares? ...There's no breaks. It just keeps going. Later.

(CHARLOTTE hangs up as the DESKCLERK's song ends. The DESKCLERK's phone rings. He picks up.)

DESKCLERK: *(On phone)* Yes...yes. The pier. Right away. I know, I know. I'll get right on it.

(DESKCLERK hangs up, goes to the overhead projector, shuffles through images, puts one up of a long desolate pier over a lake, blurry, black and white. Lanterns appear.)

12.

(On the departure board: **The pier/mother made it***)*

(Projection: A strange eyechart.)

DESKCLERK: Along the pier there are lanterns, lemon colored, glowing with an unearthly glow. Night.

Wind. Harold Boothby take something out of his jacket pocket.

(BOOTHBY *takes a sausage out of his pocket.*)

BOOTHBY: My dear sir, would you accept a sausage? My mother made it with her own hands.

(BOOTHBY *gives it to* SPELLMAN.)

SPELLMAN: Thanks, I guess.

BOOTHBY: Not at all. Take a bite.

(SPELLMAN *does. He takes another.*)

BOOTHBY: It's so good of you to share my humble food. You know, Professor Spellman, that once I regain my potency, Charlotte and I will leave the clinic. You should travel with us. Charlotte likes you. I can smell these things.

SPELLMAN: I'm afraid I...

BOOTHBY: There are trends I'm privy to, subtle shifts in the book world zeitgeist. We will partner in certain dealings, Professor Spellman. You and I. You may have information, certain Kafkaesque inklings..

SPELLMAN: I have no idea what you're talking about.

BOOTHBY: I anticipated this negative response. It's why I poisoned the sausage. You will find yourself becoming dizzy...

SPELLMAN: *(Struggling to remain vertical)* You son of a biiii...

BOOTHBY: A simple nerve relaxant. I can't permit you to get to that book before me. Whatever it is. Wherever it is.

SPELLMAN: Unnh...nggg...nggg...

BOOTHBY: This world is a crime of God's. In it, the criminal mind thrives. Regrettable, but I must accept what I've become. I have sought consolation in the wisdom of Maimonides, of Spinoza. They comfort, but they do not heal the gaping wound in the soul.

SPELLMAN: *(Hanging on to the railing)* Nuh...ngggg...

(BOOTHBY *reaches in to* SPELLMAN's *pants pocket and takes his wallet.*)

BOOTHBY: We are doomed to wait until the Lord of Hosts beckons us from beyond, where all will be revealed.

DESKCLERK: This scene, as it has so many times before, ends with the words "Goodbye, Professor Spellman".

BOOTHBY: Goodbye, Professor Spellman.

(Splash, as BOOTHBY *pushes* SPELLMAN *into the lake. The lanterns go out, one after the other. The pier is gone.)*

13.

(Departure board: **Principessa Sturdza tells Anna a number of things/Doctor Hartungen's Clinic/Riva del Garda***)*

DESKCLERK: Somewhere else in the clinic, some other time, perhaps outside the baths, in a small courtyard overgrown with flowers...

(EMILIA *crosses, carrying a tray of dirty dishes.*)

EMILIA: Dining room, scene 12.

DESKCLERK: The dining room, quiet this afternoon, except for the tiny sound of the tarot cards falling onto the formica.

(At a table, STURDZA *and* ANNA. *Nearby,* DEVRIES, *reading in his wheelchair.* STURDZA *deals tarot, a reading for* ANNA. *She turns a card.)*

STURDZA: Queen of cups—a difficult journey. Barefoot on stony ground. Rivers in flood.

(Projection: Queen of Cups.)

STURDZA: *(Turning another card)* The Ace of Wands—
the buried root. Of something. A cause.

(Projection: Ace of Wands)

STURDZA: *(Turning another card)* The Burning Tower. It
shouldn't be here. Not now.

(STURDZA *puts the card to one side, face down. It appears,
then disappears from projection.)*

STURDZA: Someone has been screwing with the deck.

DEVRIES: You'll frighten Anna with your Gypsy
nonsense.

STURDZA: Let us play our game, General. Go back to
your book.

DEVRIES: "That serene and blessed mood...a sense
sublime of something..."

STURDZA: Enough. Old soldiers always come to this.

(DR HARTUNGEN, *white doctor's coat, crosses upstage.)*

ANNA: The doctor. Should we be doing our...

(*A moment of strange breathing and stranger calisthenics as*
DR HARTUNGEN *watches. Dance. He exits, the therapeutic
dance ends, and* STURDZA *turns another card.)*

(Projection: Ten of Swords)

STURDZA: Ten of swords. The Green Man moves
through the wood. It means a lover, cherie.

ANNA: Who would want me? A girl who's so weak
some days she can barely stand, who coughs blood
onto her pillow every night. The cards lie.

STURDZA: The cards don't lie, Anna. They don't know
how.

ANNA: I'm not sure I want this lover.

STURDZA: Take what the cards offer you. Love is a pretty story. If you like it, you can keep telling it to yourself. When you discover your lover is not who you thought he was, you'll weep- but that unhappiness is only a feeling, cherie. When you grow hungry enough, you'll forget about it and eat.

ANNA: You're old, you don't hope for love anymore, so you say those things.

STURDZA: I tell you what my life has taught me.

ANNA: Do you believe in true love? *(She begins to tap the table in a steady rhythm while she waits for an answer.)*

DESKCLERK: The Principessa has to think about that one. While she does so....

(DEVRIES reads aloud to himself...)

DEVRIES: *(Reads)* "In after years,
When these wild ecstasies shall be matured
Into a sober pleasure...
Thy memory be as a dwelling-place
For all sweet sounds and..."

DESKCLERK: Boothby performs an exercise designed to activate dormant areas of the brain by imitating certain insects...

(BOOTHBY does this exercise as CHARLOTTE dials her cell...)

CHARLOTTE: *(On cell)* It's me. Yeah, I'm still at the clinic. I'll be awhile—its kinda confused around here. Look, what I'm trying to tell you is I'm pregnant... No, I am not screwing around with your head... The test doesn't lie...

ANNA: *(Repeating)* Do you believe in true love?

CHARLOTTE: *(On cell)* I'll talk to you later. There's something I gotta hear....

(CHARLOTTE hangs up, listens to STURDZA along with ANNA.)

STURDZA: One evening many years ago, I went to the
opera in Venice. I was with an Italian duke, handsome
as a god, and just as wealthy. As the audience gathered
in front of La Fenice, an old Chinese gentleman
appeared, pulling a bamboo cage on wheels. In the
cage was a black bear.

The old man took a long spoon and a jar of honey from
under his robe and fed the bear, sliding the dripping
spoon between the bars into the bear's mouth. Then he
opened the cage door. The bear shuffled out and stood
up on its hindlegs. It wore a red cap. The man talked
to it gently in Mandarin, then blew on a tiny flute.
The bear swayed in place, then began a heavy-footed
shuffle, side to side. The doors of La Fenice opened, we
threw a few coins, and went inside.

I saw them again as I was leaving Venice. The duke
had accused me of stealing an emerald necklace of his
mother's, and had called the police. I was embarking
at twilight. The bear in its cage was being hoisted by
dockside crane aboard my ship, a freighter sailing for
Morocco and Cadiz.

The Chinese gentleman watched from the dock.
Suddenly the cable snapped, and the caged bear
plunged down into the black water. The old man
howled in agony. The cage sank quickly. The red sun
followed it slowly into the Venetian lagoon, and the
first stars appeared in the darkening sky.

The Chinese gentleman boarded the ship. We sailed
off into the night and the Adriatic. I saw him at the rail
near midnight. He took his long spoon out from under
his robe, dipped it in the jar of honey, and tossed it into
the sea.

ANNA: Is that a story of true love?

STURDZA: Make of it what you will, cherie. It's true.
The bear is at the bottom of the Venetian lagoon. Fish
swim by his eyes.

14.

(CHARLOTTE *alone. She dials her cell again.*)

CHARLOTTE: *(On cell)* Bobby? ...Where'd he go? ...Who the hell is this? ...A friend of his? What's your name? ...Well, listen to me, Yvonne. That asshole better... Hello? Hello?

(SPELLMAN, *soaking wet, with a fish in his pocket, approaches her.*)

CHARLOTTE: The bitch hung up on me.

SPELLMAN: Boothby...my money...the lake. He stole my wallet. He tried to drown me.

CHARLOTTE: My sympathies. It's a wicked world.

SPELLMAN: So I've heard.

CHARLOTTE: Boothby can't help himself. A snake will bite. Forgive him. It's the only thing to do under the circumstances.

SPELLMAN: What circumstances?

CHARLOTTE: Life. Such as it is.
Oh, yeah. Here's your wallet. Boothby was dreaming, and I took it. I thought you might find me. *(She embraces him, kisses him passionately. Just as suddenly, she pulls away.)* If he discovers I'm gone, Boothby will be furious.

SPELLMAN: Charlotte, I...

CHARLOTTE: He might whip me.

SPELLMAN: Whip you?

CHARLOTTE: He does that, from time to time. When I misbehave. I have to go. *(She's gone.)*

15.

(Departure board: **#241 Rapido- Milano, Desenzano, Monte Carlo/Diane***)*

(DIANE *alone in a train compartment. She dials her cellphone.)*

DIANE *(On cell)* Jay? JAY! Pick up the damn thing. I'm not leaving a millionth fucking message...

(DIANE *hangs up, dials again.* DEAN FELDMAN *appears in another space. His cellphone rings.)*

DEAN FELDMAN: *(On cell)* Hello?

DIANE: Arthur?

DEAN FELDMAN: Diane?

DIANE: He hasn't called you, has he?

DEAN FELDMAN: I'd be the last person he'd...

DIANE: He won't answer his cell—or it's dead—or he's dead.

DEAN FELDMAN: Diane, where are you?

DIANE: Italy. On a train to Riva del Garda. Jay said he was on his way there. I'm not even sure I believe him...

DEAN FELDMAN: It makes sense, Diane. Kafka went to Riva to take the cure—baths, fresh air. A clinic.

DIANE: The book Jay dreamed about...do you...

DEAN FELDMAN: Diane, that's Jay's Kafka wet dream. Nonsense. Franz Kafka was a blabbermouth. He would have told someone—Max, Felice, or written endlessly about it in his diaries. He didn't. There is no book.

DIANE Poor baby...

DEAN FELDMAN: I feel responsible, Diane. The shock of the dismissal. He left me no choice.

DIANE: Arthur, I know Jay can be hard to reason with when he's...

DEAN FELDMAN: Look, Diane. When you come back, perhaps we could have a quiet drink somewhere. The Blue Spruce?

DIANE I guess we...

DEAN FELDMAN: Wonderful. Diane, I've always felt we had a certain connection, you and I—a kind of secret...

DIANE: Arthur, what in the world are you talking about?

DEAN FELDMAN: That lunatic doesn't deserve you! I love you. I've always...

(DIANE *hangs up.*)

DEAN FELDMAN: Diane? DIANE?

(DIANE *hangs up.* DEAN FELDMAN's *gone.*)

DIANE: Fuck.

16.

(*Departure board:* **The Dining Room/Hartungen Naturopathic Clinic/the thirsty Vrolak**)

(EMILIA *stands motionless, with a napkin over one arm. The* DESKCLERK *rings the dinnerbell. All appear for dinner,* BOOTHBY *with* CHARLOTTE, ANNA *with* STURDZA, DEVRIES, SPELLMAN, *and* DR HARTUNGEN. EMILIA *seats people, then serves.*)

STURDZA: Emilia, by the window, please.

(*She and* ANNA *are seated. They look out at the harbor.*)

STURDZA: Look, Anna! The lake at twilight. And that barque with tattered sails, the single lantern on its prow, once more entering the harbor...

After so many years, nothing has changed. You're still here, Emilia.

EMILIA: Yes, Madame. I am.

(A dead silence, as if the scene is suspended in time. Faint music. SPELLMAN joins ANNA and the Principessa.)

SPELLMAN: Principessa, what brought you here, to the clinic?

STURDZA: I was epileptic, cherie. The seizures. I saw God, then shook as a strong wind blew through me. Bite my tongue, choke on the blood and faint at last. Doctor Hartungen cured me years ago.

DEVRIES: Every man's a soldier, don't you think, Emilia?

EMILIA: So true, General.

STURDZA: I choose to remain here on the lake. When war comes, the poor fools may not trouble us here.

SPELLMAN: War? What war are you talking about?

DEVRIES: Every man—a king!

EMILIA: Very true, General.

STURDZA: Do you believe, my distinguished professore, that there are immortal creatures in these woods who spy on us for their amusement, and can bring us life or death?

SPELLMAN: What creatures? What...

STURDZA: The Vrolak, whose thirst is never satisfied, the tiny...

DR HARTUNGEN: Pardon me. Professor Spellman, I rarely forget a patient. I keep thinking you've been with us before. Some complaint of the lungs...

SPELLMAN: No, doctor. If I'd been to this clinic before, I'd remember it.

DR HARTUNGEN: One's memory is not always...a faithful servant.

DEVRIES: Every man a priest!

EMILIA: So very true, General.

ANNA: Tell me something, any of you. The sun rises every morning from the mountains beyond the lake. How can it do this—this stupid show, all pink and gold, as I bend over the sink, my chest heaving, coughing blood till my nightgown is smeared red with it... *(She takes out a bloody nightgown, holds it up.)*

STURDZA: Quiet, child.

ANNA: Look!

STURDZA: Put that away, Anna.

DR HARTUNGEN: Anna, I...

(DR HARTUNGEN falls silent. Again, the scene feels frozen in time.)

DESKCLERK: Emilia! The after-dinner drinks.

(EMILIA wheels in a rolling cart with bottles, glasses. ANNA puts the nightgown away.)

EMILIA: Brandy, whiskey, Chartreuse. The wine is Lacryma Christi, from the slopes of Vesuvius.

(EMILIA serves wine and liquor, and hands STURDZA her tarot deck.)

EMILIA: Your cards, Madame.

17.

(Departure Board: **Lacryma Christi***)*

ANNA: Read them for me.

STURDZA: Professor Spellman? Would you care to see the shadows of things to come?

ANNA: No. Tonight the deck is mine. I won't be frightened if the cards don't promise me paradise.

STURDZA: If you wish.

(STURDZA *begins to turn the cards. As she does so, their projections appear.*)

STURDZA: The Queen of Cups. Joy and harmony—a child. Three of Coins. The dark wood, *la selva oscura*. The Burning Tower. Death by fire—or a burning away—of youth, of beauty, of hope.

(*Projections: Queen of Cups/ Three of Coins/The Burning Tower*)

DEVRIES: Stop your nonsense. You're not in a caravan run by thieves.

STURDZA: Your fear is talking to us, General.

DEVRIES: I'm no longer afraid of losing anything. You're a jealous old woman. The world we live in is nightmare enough. You can at least be kind.

STURDZA: Do you want me to lie to her?

DEVRIES: The cards read many ways. The Gypsies, of all the peoples of the earth, know this to be true.

(STURDZA *is silent a long moment. Then she scoops up all the cards, restacks the deck, and sets it aside.*)

STURDZA: The Tarock will keep silent until some other evening.

(*The projection of the three cards disappears.*)

(*Projection: a chart of a healing dance, with footprints.*)

DESKCLERK: Healing dance, number nineteen!

(*All dance. Fabulous finish.* STURDZA *collapses into a chair.*)

STURDZA: Emilia, bring me a brandy.

(EMILIA *does so. On the departure board:* **Villa Aldobrandini and its marble steps/ Pontius Pilate.**)

ANNA: I'm going walking by the lake.

DR HARTUNGEN: Open the iron gate, go through the arch, and the path leads all the way to the Villa Aldobrandini. You can sit on the marble steps, and Lago di Garda will lap at your feet.

(ANNA *walks toward the doorway.*)

SPELLMAN: I'll go with you...if you don't mind.

ANNA: Then don't just sit there.

(SPELLMAN *stands, catches up to* ANNA. *As they exit,* ANNA *turns back.*)

ANNA: Are you really a Gypsy?

STURDZA: Full blood, cherie. My mother was Romanian, my father a Turk from Izmir on the Black Sea. He was a great lover of garlic and women, with a huge moustache.

(ANNA *and* SPELLMAN *are gone.*)

DR HARTUNGEN: Is that Gypsy story true? You told me you were White Russian, from Minsk.

STURDZA: What is truth, Doctor?

(EMILIA *begins to clear away bottles and glasses.*)

EMILIA: The Bible teaches that Pontius Pilate asked the Christ that same question.

STURDZA: Did he now? What a coincidence.

18.

(*Departure board:* 'I he marble steps/ Lago di Garda)

DESKCLERK: Spellman and Anna are on the marble steps of the villa. The surface of the lake is still, a sheet of black glass. Shooting stars.

ANNA: Look! The stars are falling! There goes one. And another!

SPELLMAN: A meteor shower.

ANNA: They leave those curving trails of starlight...

SPELLMAN: It happens this time of year.

ANNA: There's another! And another one! Soon the stars will all be gone, fallen into the lake. The sky will be up there all alone, black and empty.
There's another!

19.

(Departure board: **General Devries answers some questions***)*

*(*DEVRIES *in his wheelchair alone. A candle. Distant thunder)*

DESKCLERK: It's late. Everyone at the clinic has gone to bed. With one exception. There's been thunder off and on for hours, and at last it begins to rain.

(The DESKCLERK'*s light goes out.* DEVRIES *is alone. Sound of rain)*

(Out of the darkness, DR HARTUNGEN*)*

DR HARTUNGEN: You should be in bed.

DEVRIES: The thunder woke me.

DR HARTUNGEN: I've been observing you lately, General. You spend your days watching the smoke rising from the burning tip of your cigarette. Or reading Wordsworth, the most bloodless poet ever to live. You no longer follow my exercise prescriptions. Why don't you go home to be with your family? You have grandchildren...

DEVRIES: They've forgotten me long ago. I've been a soldier, and then a wanderer. I've lived in Shanghai, London, San Francisco. I married three times, and had a number of pointless affairs. The friends I once had are dead now. I prefer it here.

DR HARTUNGEN: You should write a memoir, general.

DEVRIES: I have no interest in memories, my own or anyone else's.

DR HARTUNGEN: That's a lie. We are all slaves to the past, either in sorrow and regret—wishing it undone— or in longing—to bring back moments that can never return.

DEVRIES: There is an incident from my life that might interest you, doctor.

I first stayed in Riva del Garda when I was fifty-five, not yet an old man. I was at the Hotel du Parc. There was a young couple, English. The husband was painting a view of the village from the lake-- some sort of artist.

He was out on the water all day, with his easel mounted in a rowboat. His wife was bored, reading in the hotel garden. She was one of those English women, slim, delicate, with a flush that never left her cheek. A blonde. Her hair was long, tied up in a sort of twist in the back. I invited her to walk up to an abandoned church in the mountains. She agreed. We were sweating, climbing the steep trail. We reached the ruin at last. Far below on the lake, we could see the tiny figure of her husband in his boat. She untied her blonde hair and shook it out. It fell halfway down her back, and around her face. I kissed her. She tasted like sweet peppermint mixed with sweat. As our lips met, a bird cried from the church roof. There must have been a nest in the broken tiles.

She was surprised I kissed her, an older man, and a stranger. She said something, I forget what. Then she smiled at me a moment, and went back down the hill alone. I watched her until she disappeared among the trees. I thought of going into the church to pray, but the building was locked.

In the morning, I arrived in the breakfast room promptly at seven, and dawdled forever over my coffee. The English couple did not appear.

I learned at the front desk that they had checked out. A car had come at five a.m. to take them to the train in Desenzano. I never learned her name.

Every season for twenty years I returned to the Hotel du Parc, hoping that she would also. A few years ago I became ill. I realized I could stay at this clinic and walk to the grounds of the hotel. It's only a few minutes away, near the ferry.

When she returns, do you think she'll know me? Years have passed, after all. Perhaps she's no longer married. Of course, she'd be over forty by now. She may have had children. Perhaps they'll come with her and build sandcastles by the shore...

(DR HARTUNGEN *is weeping.*)

DEVRIES: Please. I need no pity from anyone. I have none for myself. Don't cry for me.

DR HARTUNGEN: I'm crying for us all.

DEVRIES: In that case, my dear doctor, let the teardrops fall.

20.

(Departure board: **A conversation by the shore/the Choirmaster***)*

(SPELLMAN *and* DR HARTUNGEN *by the lake shore. A bench)*

SPELLMAN: Tell me something, doctor. Anything. Have you found Kafka's novel? Discovered it isn't there? Has the search even begun? It seems like I've been here for weeks...

DR HARTUNGEN: Why are you in such a hurry to leave us?

SPELLMAN: I can't stay here forever. I have another life—my wife, my work...

(From a distance, the sound of a children's choir, singing a hymn.)

DR HARTUNGEN: Do you hear them? The children's choir in the village. I've sent Emilia to...

(EMILIA *enters.)*

DR HARTUNGEN: Ah! Did you see the choirmaster?

EMILIA: The choirmaster cursed at me. In front of the children. He was enraged you would suggest they miss choir practice to...

DR HARTUNGEN: Go on.

EMILIA: ...to search rat-infested tunnels for some fool's book that turned to dust long ago.

(EMILIA *is gone. The choir fades.)*

DR HARTUNGEN: Now you know the kind of petty, arrogant, selfish people we have to deal with in the village. All the children spend their after-school hours at choir. Without them...the storage tunnels are low and narrow, and go for miles...

SPELLMAN: Just... just find the damn thing for me.
Whatever it is. Or isn't. Just let me... *(He falls silent. He
sits down on the bench.)*

DR HARTUNGEN: I will talk to the choirmaster
personally. As soon as possible. Tomorrow. Or the day
after... *(He leaves quietly.)*

(SPELLMAN *alone. He looks out at the lake.)*

21.

(Departure board: **Wordsworth/lemon trees***)*

*(*DEVRIES *in his chair, with his book of poetry.* EMILIA *is
nearby.)*

EMILIA: Will there be anything else, general?

DEVRIES: No, Emilia. You can go.

(EMILIA *doesn't move. As* DEVRIES *speaks, other mourners
enter:* DR HARTUNGEN, SPELLMAN, STURDZA, ANNA.*)*

DEVRIES: Wet spring smell of the lemon trees...smoke
rising from a cigarette...the curve of her lips...that
garden near Finsbury, Queen Anne roses, warm wind
off the sea... "If I should be where I...no more can hear
thy voice..."

DESKCLERK: The general's book falls to the floor. The
mourners' clothes flutter in the rising wind off the lake.
And so it happens....

22.

(Departure board: **On Lago di Garda***)*

(Projection: the lake)

(SPELLMAN *and* ANNA *in a rowboat.* SPELLMAN *rows,*
ANNA *in the stern.)*

SPELLMAN: Anna, are you...dangerously ill?

ANNA: What are you asking? Will I...

SPELLMAN: No, I... Sorry. I'm so sorry.

ANNA: It doesn't matter.

SPELLMAN: I shouldn't have...

(A silence between them.)

SPELLMAN: Anna, why are you here?

ANNA: To heal myself, of course. Like everyone else.

SPELLMAN: Everyone else is older. They seem like they've been here forever.

ANNA: The truth is—I'm only here because of you. I knew somehow you'd be here. I made my aunt bring me. You haven't seen her. She keeps to her room, even for meals. She's very pale, just sits in bed and looks out the window at the lake. She doesn't know what I do all day. I tell her I'm taking walks in the hills. Today I'll tell her I went as far as Vernaccia, and had a gelato limone in the square.

(A silence between them.)

ANNA: Why did you come here?

SPELLMAN: A book. Something about a book. Anna, I.... *(He falls silent.)*

ANNA: The trouble is in my lungs. I cough blood in the mornings, before breakfast. It wakes me at night. I lie there in pain, staring at the cracks in the ceiling of my room.
Do you think I'll live or die?

SPELLMAN: I don't know.

ANNA: How could you? Anyway, it doesn't matter.

SPELLMAN: Don't keep saying that.

ANNA: I'll say what I like.

(Boat horn far away. Silence between them. The boat drifts.)

SPELLMAN: I love you, Anna.

ANNA: Without you, Franz, I don't know how I'll live.

SPELLMAN: What did you say?

ANNA: You heard me very well.
Shall I take off my clothes? Do you want to see me
naked? I'm quite pretty, really...except for a tiny scar.

23.

(Departure board: **Anna goes home/toujours la meme
chose***)*

(Boat horn. STURDZA *and* SPELLMAN*)*

(Projection: The lake)

STURDZA: Doctor Hartungen is sending Anna away.
She is going back, to her other life. He can do no more
for her.
She will die, or she will live on, and do what people do.

(In the distance is ANNA, *on a ferryboat. She waves.)*

(The image of ANNA *fades into darkness. She's gone. From a
distance, the boat horn.)*

*(*SPELLMAN *is crying.)*

STURDZA: Stop crying, and I'll tell you something to
amuse you. Our Doctor Hartungen is a shameless
lecher. I saw him in the village the other day, near the
Hotel du

Parc. That Turkish girl who sells figs in the Piazza
Brolo was caressing his penis under the arcade. No one
noticed but me, as I have an eye for such goings on. *Le
monde, cherie—toujours la meme chose.*

24.

(Departure board: **Diane/Riva del Garda***)*

(The imposing door to the clinic with its brass knob. Nearby, DIANE *looks around.)*

DESKCLERK: Once again, the harbor at Riva.

DIANE: Two boys play at dice near the ferry dock. A Turkish girl sells figs under the arcade.

DESKCLERK: Did you say figs, or pigs?

DIANE: A flock of doves bursts suddenly from a rooftop. The owner of a lakeside cafe puts his head down on a table and dreams.

(The DESKCLERK *puts his head down on his table.)*

*(*DIANE *approaches the door hesitantly, knocks. No answer. She knocks again.* BOOTHBY *appears suddenly from behind her, dragging* CHARLOTTE *by one wrist.)*

BOOTHBY: There's no need to knock. We're all on the same side of the door.
I'm Harold Boothby, my niece Charlotte.

CHARLOTTE: Let go of me!

DIANE: Is this the Hartungen clinic?

BOOTHBY: You must be Diane Spellman.

DIANE: How do you know my...

BOOTHBY: We're intimate friends of your husband's. The man is an inveterate liar.

DIANE: Look, whatever your relationship with him is, I just need to find him. He...

BOOTHBY: I'll take you into the clinic personally, but first...

*(*BOOTHBY *tapes* CHARLOTTE's *hands to the brass doorknob, rips off her shirt. She's in her bra. He takes out a whip.)*

BOOTHBY: I'm sorry you have to see this, Diane, but Charlotte has misbehaved once too often.

CHARLOTTE: Don't worry. It doesn't hurt that much. Really.

(BOOTHBY *cracks the whip, with a flourish.*)

CHARLOTTE: Just close your eyes, Diane. Don't look!

BOOTHBY: Charlotte! Silence!

(*A moment of silence*)

BOOTHBY: Punishment is better in the dark.

DESKCLERK: Lights OUT! NOW!

(*Blackout*)

(*Sound of the whip.* CHARLOTTE *screams. The whip again.*)

DIANE: No! Stop!

(*The whip again. Another scream, and sobbing. The sobbing fades.*)

DESKCLERK: Lights up, please.

(*The lights come back on suddenly.* CHARLOTTE *is untied, dressed, reading her copy of "The Trial."* BOOTHBY *coils his whip. Then he reaches into his pocket, takes out a lipstick.*)

BOOTHBY: Flamingo pink, a color that suits a woman a bit past her prime. I own a cosmetics factory in Austria. The formula for the lipstick—a family secret. The ten thousand sensitive nerve endings in a woman's lips must be protected. (*He hands the lipstick to* DIANE.) My gift.
But lipstick's strictly a sideline. I'm a principal of Boothby and Montague, rare editions.
Where, exactly, is that book, Mrs Spellman? The one your husband is so desperate to find.

DIANE: My husband's delusional. Obsessed. There is no book.

BOOTHBY: Lies, Diane! The book! Kafka's book! Where is it? What story does it tell?

(All are silent.)

BOOTHBY: From an unscrupulous and half- senile bookdealer on Tottenham Court Road we received this distorted description. Charlotte!

CHARLOTTE: A novel set in Trieste, concerning a demented student, Joseph O, and an all-girl Yiddish theatrical troupe, led by the well-endowed and enigmatic Sasha Rabinowitz.

BOOTHBY: More lies!

CHARLOTTE: Pay no attention to Boothby. He...

(BOOTHBY grabs DIANE roughly by the arm.)

BOOTHBY: Join me on the pier over the lake. The night sky, the lights of the little villages, the silhouette of the abandoned church. The fresh air will calm your fevered mind.

(BOOTHBY hauls DIANE out after him. They're gone. CHARLOTTE shrugs, turns again to "The Trial.")

25.

(Departure board: **The Pier/Honi soit qui mal y pense***)*

(The pier again, the projection, the lanterns, the strange eyechart.)

DESKCLERK: The pier over the lake. Night. Wind. The lanterns, lemon colored, glowing with an unearthly glow. Once again, Boothby reaches into his jacket pocket...

BOOTHBY: Please. Accept a sausage. My mother made it with her own hands. Have a bite.

DIANE: No thanks. I'm vegetarian.

(BOOTHBY *shrugs, tosses the sausage off the pier, grabs* DIANE *tightly.*)

BOOTHBY: You're an attractive woman, Mrs Spellman. You and I, we can share the money, lead an extremely upscale life together. For the last time—tell me exactly what book your husband is searching for, and its exact location.

DIANE: I don't know where it is, or what it is.

BOOTHBY: These lies are horribly unwelcome. Doesn't the name Kafka mean anything to you?

DIANE: Wasn't he the one who wrote that weird story about the bug?

BOOTHBY: Mrs Spellman, please be kind enough to get naked and lie down on the pier. We will have raw sex as the lake rolls on beneath us. In your ecstasy, you will stop lying and reveal your secrets.

DIANE: You are completely batshit crazy.

BOOTHBY: Your presence in this story is no longer necessary.

(BOOTHBY *attempts to pick up* DIANE *and throw her off the pier into the lake. They struggle, she trips him, he loses his balance, and she pushes him over the low railing, off the pier into the lake. Splash! He screams, and the scream fades...*)

(DIANE *looks down into the water at the disappearing form of* BOOTHBY.)

DIANE: Fuck this.

26.

(Departure board: **Tea leaves***)*

(The clinic, in the Music Room. Music, softly. Chopin.
CHARLOTTE *stares out the window, her book in her lap. A
disheveled* DIANE *enters.* CHARLOTTE *looks her over.)*

CHARLOTTE: Welcome to the clinic.

DIANE: The front door was open. I just walked in.

CHARLOTTE: Where's Boothby?

DIANE: I couldn't help it. He...

CHARLOTTE: You threw Boothby off the pier?

DIANE: He was trying to kill me. I didn't mean to...

CHARLOTTE: Please. He has remarkable powers of
recovery. He'll be back, wet and angry. He'll take it out
on me.

DIANE: I had to...

CHARLOTTE: Boothby is merciless. He'll whip me again.
Then he'll leave me.
What can I do?

DIANE: I have no idea. I...

CHARLOTTE: The question was rhetorical. I'll go back to
tealeaf reading.

DIANE: Do you tell the future?

CHARLOTTE: The leaves do that. I just read them.
I learned when I was quite young, and I had the gift
for it. I say I'm Austrian, or English, but I was born
in Moldavia, in Jassy. My father was a violinist in the
Moldavian Opera orchestra. During the intermezzo he
would sneak into the checkroom and go through the
coat pockets. They caught him, put him in prison. My
mother sold her jewelry and bought us train tickets to
Paris. An enormously rich man took care of us there, in

a beautiful apartment on the Place Dauphine. He lost
all his money at the tables. Chemin de fer. My mother
taught me to read the tea leaves, then abandoned me
in the Luxembourg Gardens, by the carousel. She went
into a convent in Montpellier. I believe she's still there.
A few years later, at a tearoom in Rue Saint Honoré, I
met Boothby. I was sixteen. I read his cup.
The leaves foretold a beautiful future for the two of us
if I ran away with him.

(DIANE *and* CHARLOTTE *sit quietly.* CHARLOTTE *lights a
cigarette. The music plays on.*)

27.

(*Departure Board:* **Time in Kafka**)

(*Somewhere in the clinic.* SPELLMAN *in a chair,* EMILIA
standing nearby. He holds a notebook.)

SPELLMAN: In this notebook is the story of my search
for Kafka's lost novel, all in my clumsy longhand.
Perhaps I can leave it here with you, Emilia. I'll be back
for it someday, after the war...

EMILIA: Of course. (*She takes the notebook.*)

SPELLMAN: I've been here before, haven't I?

(EMILIA *doesn't answer. She exits.* SPELLMAN *is alone.*)

SPELLMAN: Doctor? Doctor Hartungen?
I want to go now. Home. To my wife.

(DR HARTUNGEN *is revealed in the shadows. He comes
forward.*)

DR HARTUNGEN: You're not well. Stay here, with Anna.

SPELLMAN: Anna's gone.

(*The sound of the children's choir in the distance, singing a
hymn.*)

DR HARTUNGEN: She'll return. To find you. Or
someone very like her will return. The general's coffin
will once again be carried to the graveyard on the hill.
Principessa Sturdza will turn over the Queen of Cups.
I'll be here.

I spoke to the choirmaster, and the entire children's
choir has joined the search. A hundred children with
electric torches are in the storage tunnels. We may find
the book today. Or tomorrow...

SPELLMAN: I don't care anymore. Let me go.

DR HARTUNGEN: Our clinic has treated Magnus
Hirschfeld, Cesare Lombroso, Thomas Mann. Franz
Kafka as well.

A sick man. He stayed up far too many nights,
sleepless, with a migraine, walking around the lake,
soaking up moonlight....

His book may be nothing but hypochondria, vanity...
Not a book Dr. Kafka wanted to give the world.

So tired, you're so tired. Just take your rest

(DR HARTUNGEN *exits quietly.* SPELLMAN *alone in his
chair, eyes closed.*)

28.

(*Departure board:* **Departure/Diane**)

(SPELLMAN *remains in his chair. All around him the clinic
slowly fades away into darkness as the ethereal singing of the
children's choir rises. He sits up, looks out...*)

SPELLMAN: They're leaving me—Anna, the Principessa,
General Devries, Emilia—led by Doctor Hartungen in
his white coat, a book under his arm. They're beyond
the lake, going over the mountains. There they are on
the horizon... They're gone.

(*The choir fades into silence.*)

DIANE: *(O S)* Jay? Jay?

(DIANE *enters, approaches* SPELLMAN. *The clinic has disappeared.*)

DIANE: Jay? It's me. I'm here.

SPELLMAN: Diane? You can't be here. You...

DIANE: I came to find you. To take you home.

(SPELLMAN *stands unsteadily, then embraces* DIANE.)

SPELLMAN: I'm so glad, Diane. So glad...

(DIANE *holds* SPELLMAN *close.*)

29.

(*Departure board:* **Back in the U S A/A cafe/Kir**)

(*A cafe.* DEAN FELDMAN *and* DIANE. *Two kirs. In another space,* SPELLMAN *looks over some papers.*)

DIANE: Jay was delirious, Arthur, but he knew me. He was just sitting in the burned out shell of what was once this sanitarium by the lake, long ago...

DEAN FELDMAN: The Hartungen Naturopathic Clinic.

DIANE: Where Kafka stayed. It closed in the twenties, then became the Hotel du Lac. The building burned in the fires around the lake last autumn. No one's there anymore. Just fireflies, floating through the ruins in the evening.

DEAN FELDMAN: How is he now, Diane?

DIANE: Much better. They say he'll make a full recovery, with time. Arthur, hire him back. He can teach, I know it. It's what he needs.

DEAN FELDMAN: Diane, you live in your own dream, like Jay. Inside your dream, you love him, and you

live in this college town, and that's your life. In the
evening, the fireflies float through the ruins.
I can wake you, set you free. We'll go to Prague...

DIANE: I won't go to Prague with you, Arthur. Or to
bed.

DEAN FELDMAN: More's the pity. Another kir?

DIANE: I don't think so.

DEAN FELDMAN: I'll have one. And I'll hire him back,
for your sake.

30.

(Departure board: **Asst. Professor Spellman lectures/a
college, U S A***)*

(SPELLMAN *lectures to his students.)*

SPELLMAN: Anna heals rapidly at home. She comes
back to Riva in the spring, stays at a small pensione.
Franz is nowhere to be found.
At night Anna wades into Lake Garda, and the cold
water laps at her swelling belly. She's pregnant with
Doctor Kafka's child. The moon is yellow as butter, and
the stars fall again in long slow arcs toward the lake...
Franz is gone, gone back to Prague to write letters
to Felice, to cough blood. Anna is a diary entry, a
whispered conversation with Max, a memory...
She returns to Riva del Garda one more time, in
August 1925. Franz has died at another clinic, this one
at Kierling in Austria, though she doesn't know this,
and still hopes to see him walking along the path by
the lake. Anna sits by the shore and watches her son,
now twelve years old, dive off the pier below the Hotel
du Lac, and swim in the dark water.

Time in Kafka is always broken. Every moment leads back to itself, infinite with echoes, chronological and eternal.

Any questions from the peanut gallery?

Then that's it, boys and girls.

(*Lights fade on* SPELLMAN, *and up on the* DESKCLERK *near his table and projector. He finds the image he needs, blurry, black and white....*)

(*Projection: a sprawling building overlooking a lake. Soothing music.*)

(*The* DESKCLERK *sits, notices the audience, speaks into his microphone.*

DESKCLERK: Welcome to the clinic.

Name? Name?

(*Lights to black*)

END OF PLAY